Bangkok
and the nights of drunken stupor

Scott Shaw

Buddha Rose Publications

First Edition 1988
Second Edition 2008
Third Edition 2009
Fourth Edition 2025

ISBN: 1-877792-06-3
ISBN-13: 978-1877792069

Library of Congress Cataloging in Publication Data:
Bangkok and the Nights of Drunken Stupor
1. Bangkok (Thailand) – Poetry
2. I. Title
PS3569.H38627B3 1989
811' .54 – dc 20

Library of Congress Catalog Card Number:
89-23884

10 9 8 7 6 5 4 3 2 1
Printed in the United States of America

Bangkok
and the nights of drunken stupor

To:

Manita S.
and all her lies,
Pichitra D.
and her white powder truths,
and mostly to the Goddess
who has permeated my soul
and left me with Siam vision

one

are you waiting for me
waiting before I come
are you waiting for me tonight
as the drunken air of 35,000 feet
surrounds me

is your soul
lost in false contentment
that I am almost there
so limiting, so lost
do you long to hold me
as I long to hold you
could it be that you love me
or could it be only the game we both play
the dream we dream

do you desire to hold me
or am I to you
as you are to me
just another chance
in the dance
the dance that I do so well

could it be mere moments
      lost in dream of passion
      lost to wars of our time

time to times
war to wars
again death confronts us

      death to me
      death to you
      death to us

and again I must cast them off

cast off the demons of demise
        cast them off
        with simply an
        oh well…

two

korean woman
waiting for me
seoul city
japanese girl
waiting for me
tokyo night
spanish lady
waiting for me
L.A.
are they in themselves the answer
or just deepening parts
to an ever-more lost puzzle

> as I sit here
> the beginning
> the first night
> of intoxication
>
> *bangkok...*

three

earrings
      in my hand
earrings
      in my pocket
earring
      that I have removed
      from my ears
      trying to fit into
      a world I never could

torn between
society and myself
a fool's choice
in a fool's world

four

can you forgive me
for a moment
a moment
in our time
can you hold me
just a minute longer
can you hold me
just a minute more

five

mud
of miles unspoken
sewer ridden streets
colored in
rainy sky
they leave me stranded
standing here staring
a sight so common
yet so unknown

> hold me golden goddess
> hold me, as this day
> becomes this night
> sing to me
> all of the songs
> that you have sung before
> but this time
> sing them to me

there is not any reason
for confessions
no reason to pretend

a confessed sin
is only a sin to the self

golden arm/golden hand
I turned around in these streets
they left me standing
standing alone
left me here, alone
being only who I am

six

cast to thai demons
held by a whore
in a thai night
left to the ashes
of cremation fire
left to the east

singing golden statue
dancing in the night
prayed-for distant messenger
unfold your knowledge
lay it out before me

      it remains
            unforgettable

rhythm-to-rhythm
prayer-to-prayer
answered in aborted idolism
thrown in
      to a lost
      non-monotheistic night

and then
the religion was gone…

seven

addiction
so long ago lost
but so long held onto

love/lust

cry to me in my night
by morning
cry to me again

a song worth singing
a song never left unsung

eight

will I find you when I wake
      will I find a dream
will tomorrow be spoken for
      or will it be just another day

nine

oh yes
thank you very kindly
no more
too much to handle

       and the circle turns
       and the letters send
       and tomorrow's dream
       become just another
       forgotten memory

ten

well, I put my sport coat on
and out the door
      to the streets
I went

no city heat tonight
nothing to attract me

      if it's there this evening
      I can find it

so here I am
stuck with my words

      such as they are

left with the dreams and the memories
of how special Taipei was
the last time around

but still
here I am
in a rapidly sobering state

      stayed up way past the point of tired
      now wide awake

bangkok time
nothing to do
except listen to piano bar music
through my hotel room door
and eventually go to sleep
and dream of the dancing

eleven

I want to be sleeping with you

      my clothes
           they are off
      I have eaten the hotel choco-late
      I wish you could have fed it to me
           before bed

      king-sized bed

I wish I could have fed it to you

ah…
but in time
perhaps
it will be my wish
to be away from you
because that's just who I am

but mow
to feed you chocolate
to caress your bronze body
and to hold you

      my current fantasy
      I will live you

           soon

twelve

poems I have written
dreams I have fed
as I sit here
another bangkok evening
      late evening
having just finished
a $300.00 bottle of wine

      I have played this game so well
      too well, maybe

      I always take it past
      that final limit

      where-else is anything learned
      where-else is anything gained

one more journey
to birth or death
      time and experience will tell
do I care which
I don't think so
no, not much

so should I step out further
step into the bangkok night
      yes ?
      no ?
no time…
almost daylight
so just go to sleep
and remember to forget
forget, the obscure
forget, undefined pain of today

thirteen

may I say something to you ?
even though I know
      you must be,
      you are,
      spoken for

I must tell you
that of all my journeys to thailand
you are the most beautiful women
I have ever seen

      lie-to-lie
      bed-to-bed
      get her into mine

a kiss for the dream
a kiss for the lie
nothing equals anything
just a night lived
for whatever it was worth

fourteen

leave another heart bleeding
leave
with a reason to return
this party has gotten
so expensive
and I am afraid it is about to end

      so cry a little tear for me
      when I leave you standing alone
      give me another look
      to place upon my wall

      hold me, tell me that you love me
      I'll tell you how I love you too
            how I want
                  how I wish, I could

      drift to disillusions
      of immature grandeur
      a choice made
      all by ourselves

      nothing to do
      nothing left to feel
      and certainly
      nothing left to lose

      just know that there is a game
      and play it well

      play it well
      I play it too well

fifteen

sun-to-sun
feel the music
of the rain each afternoon
listen to its movement
as it casts its spell

      a reason to live
            a reason to die

and when there is nothing left
        it gives me a reason to become

sixteen

I could walk off
if only I had the strength
I could live one more
but I do not know the way
so I sit here
intoxicated
one more evening
one more dream
one more lost reality
in a world not worth knowing

seventeen

euphoria
articulate euphoria
it only lasts a second
one minute
in our life
what could it be worth ?

eighteen

+ 500
I drunkenly write
the first night

+ 700
I drunkenly write
the second night

       how much ?
       how cheap ?

       in american mind
       in thai money

I wish I knew
but what I wish more is to touch the hostess tonight

nineteen

will it be the same
will it be better
will I take you to hundred dollar
bottle of wine dinners
and to hundred dollar a day
hotel rooms in the night
could I/will I
I have for those before

will you be another reason
perhaps another style
perhaps even another sin
will your truth mean more to me
or will your lies be all the same

live with me in a fool's illusion
in a fool's lonely dream
kiss me/touch me
give me all you have
for what comes tomorrow
certainly I do not know
but what can be lived in this moment
this moment,
where nothing else may be known
this moment,
is certainly understood by me
I give it here to you
a gift for a gift
time spend at my expense
a time worth giving
a gift worth receiving
this gift I bestow upon you

twenty

does tonight's wine hold me back
does it hold me tight
     in its arms
         its fleeting arms
will it let me leave
give me reason to go
back to my terrain/my territory
the darkness of the deadly streets

     the streets
     the place where I grew up
     the place where I live
     the people I embrace
     the people I know
         I understand/I hate

     I will go again
     put myself in their midst
     the street/the people
     who hold onto unlived dreams
     unknown truths
     forgotten realities

     a kiss of passion
     a desire for death
     yes, I will go there
     how can I remain anywhere else

the wine and its reasons
the wine and its lies
its ability to deceive
its ability to create
its fleeting arms of desire
they grab me

hold me so tight
they give me the reason
the ability to dream

they give me the reason
the ability to lie

pour your grace down my throat
let me live this illusion

forever

       forever and ever and ever

twenty-one

drink, just the right amount
the most expensive wine on the menu
eat, European style
leave just a little food on the plate

all in the game
the game, as all games go
> the game I fit into
> and play so well

> speak to me
> of your fantasies
> speak to me
> in your rhythms
> listen to me
> with eyes of darkness
> as I raise my hand

> spread your legs
> make love to me
> Southeast Asian girl
> hold me tight
> hold me long

> look up/look at me
> I look at you
> then I spit in your face
>> it's all just sadly
>> who I am
>> and it's all just sadly
>> who you have become

> a lover, I thought was a lover
> a lover, who turned out to be a whore

twenty-two

go to sleep
intoxicated mood
will I wake to the day
or will I wake to the night

      day becomes night
      lost in drunken stupor

a bangkok star
stared back at me
another star
another star to forget

infested
deep lost forgotten
drunken night/drunken reason
written words/spoken lies

another kiss goodnight
      another kiss goodbye

twenty-three

take a room
for the night
I'll take it where you work
take it for the experience of passion
I'll take it
for whatever it is worth
       and then I will say goodbye

I have long imagined
what I would say
what I would do
but it is more than all of that
being here
       wrapped/trapped
in your caramel flavored arms
being here
       tied
in your caramel flavored love

intoxicated
it's all a poet's dream

because I don't know your name
I'll just call you bangkok

       thank you, bangkok
       thank you for the opportunity
       to live the dream

twenty-four

another word
        for another night
I finished it with a cognac
a gift from Marco
        Marco, the maitre d'

        but it brought back
        too many remembrances
        of too much recently consumed
        Jack Daniels whiskey

I want to throw up
it took all I had to get even a few drops down

I sit here, sick
in the bangkok night

ah, bangkok
        with every dance
                there is another chance

twenty-five

do you have the grace for passion
come in
don't say a word
just lay down

twenty-six

it's now 2:00 A.M.
it may just a s well be 4:00 A.M.
I sit/I wait
       I await a dream
       I await a vision
       I await another reason to pretend

I could go out
go out and get a hooker
you know I have some time to kill
but today
as I walked the streets
a trampy little
would be/wanta be/will be
whore
fourteen-ish
playing her little game
came up behind me
       close behind me
followed me as I walked

and once again
       I am reminded

       it seems I so often forget

that a whore is just a whore
so thank you
but no thank you
not tonight

twenty-seven

I missed you today bronze goddess
but it is just a chance
to meet on another day

> forced existence
> I peer through thailand's haze
> and I see that here
> > I am truly free

so thailand, my friend
though the smell of your streets
> sometimes gets old
> somewhat reminiscent of mother india
and the traffic/your traffic
the cars/your cars
hours and hours
of what should only take five minutes
> the noise
> > too much noise
your noise
but it is all you

and yes
you do have a lack of fashion-passion
but that will come in time
and yes
you have more than semi-beautiful women
who love to check my form
and your blatant Buddhism
orange everywhere
and your streets
ah, your streets
they keep me coming back
see you another day

twenty-eight

she walked straight up to me
pointed at my umbrella
she looked a bit unusual for b'kok
almost east indian

as she walked closer
she stretched out her arm
and without even a thought
I handed my umbrella to her

> handed it to here
> in the pouring
> Southeast Asian rain

I watched as she walked away

> in just a few seconds
> I was soaked

I though of the money in pocket
and how I had see umbrellas for sale
but I just laughed
and choose to let the divine rain of bangkok
rain on me

> *ah, bangkok*

twenty-nine

I'll send you a letter
perhaps a letter packed in a box
a box of my remaining things
a box of my remains
perhaps in that letter
you will find
all of my remaining desires
all of my remaining tears
all that I have left behind
for perhaps in that space
the space of all perhaps-ness
I will die
choose to die
in Southeast Asia
in a Southeast Asian way

      I see a scene
      a scene of trees – vegetation
      a river flowing by
      a muddy river
      a Southeast Asian river
      perhaps it is there
      perhaps in that scene
      the scene in all its perhaps-ness
      I will make the choice
      enter into total freedom
      total abyss of nothing
      nothing that matter at all
      the total abyss of no-thing-ness
      perhaps it will be that way
      perhaps in all the perhaps-ness
      to die in Southeast Asia

I'll send you a letter
perhaps a letter packed into a box

thirty

five beers down
my mind begins to feel it
love, possible love
sitting next to me
I think so...

      in a maneuver
      beyond maneuvers
      I let her move to me

thirty-one

I spend my time lost and waiting
      lost in malignant dispassion
            sitting in perpetual passion

dispassion for this/passion for that
it can only arise in
what is not
and not in
what is

plastered to the passion
cast to the dispassion
I am left moving
dancing
holding my own
in a world with no mind

thirty-two

I see you walk out of an expensive hotel room
I see the distaste in your eyes
distaste for the night you have just spent
distaste for who you are
what the world has made you

life and time
it all flows together
as you dream of someone to finally love you
to take you away
from this land
the dream continues
but it is supplemented
by the money in your hand
the money in your pocket
money from the bed
you lay your back upon

spend it wisely…

thirty-three

I feel the hot breath of passion
breathing down my neck
I feel the hot breath of passion
in the hot bangkok night

infractions/attractions
eyes meets eyes
as the sun dims slowly
"Hey honey," she says
"Come over here."
      come I go
      as cum, I will
      what else can a guy like me do ?

infractions/retractions
nothing remains sacred
in the steaming heat of the night
that is coming on

if I had a reason to walk away
the truth is I probably would
but when no answer lives in the visions ahead
the momentary truth proves self-evident

      a lie that is lived
      is a lie that is known
      only the truth emerges untouched

so I walked to her
touched her gently
loved her softly
I loved her as if I truly did

but when all that is gone
is all that is known
and the scream for freedom
is the scream for reason
nothing can remain unbound

a kiss of attraction
becomes a love of distraction
it can only last for its moment

I feel the hot breath of passion
breathing down my neck
I feel the hot breath of passion
in the hot bangkok night

thirty-four

I kiss
lips of lust
as they slowly touch mine
I stepped into them
I stepped beyond them
but it was I
who chose to go for the ride

hold onto it
pull away from it
the ladies of the night grab my arm

       pay the price
       what is the price ?
       the price, unfortunately
       in never quite clear

live it/end it
it is all the same
in a moment it will all be forgotten
in a moment it will not matter at all

lies and promises
a touch that is forgotten too soon
a lie that lives
is truth only in a fool's mind
wake up
and it is gone

passed onto the moments
moments of fruitless willingness

if only life were different
and time did not paint our minds

but time, it is sad
dictates all that lives
every moment of hello
holds in its grasp
the sad kiss of goodbye

      eyes that are painted
      the different patterns
      that make up the night
      they see me
      they do all they can to hold me
      but nothing can remain forever
      just as nothing
      can ever stay the same

thirty-five

as the notes sounded
     a few perhaps
       were a bit out of key
as the notes sounded
     a few perhaps
       were a bit too loud
but the moment was there
fate was sealed
our eyes met, remembering
       trying to remember
           from where/from when

but where or when
it did not seem so important
as the notes slowly wept
once again into the night

into the night
another night of passion
as I undressed you
I remembered the notes
you gently played upon the piano

play those notes again
play them gently
play them upon me

thirty-six

it started out
my seeking slight intoxication
the hot evening wore on
> into the room came
> a passion filled dancer
> a dreamer in a thai dress

she sang to me
of her beliefs
danced for me her lies
painted for me
her reasons for obsession

> any desire
> is sufficient desire
> for a dancer to believe

note-to-note
touch-to-touch
in the moment of passion
we became one

but as all dreamers know
sooner or later
one always wakes up
> I woke to find
> that she had gone
> without even saying goodbye

the perfect love affair

thirty-seven

woman from the hills
as I look out the window
I see your reflection
and the stars in the sky

woman in my room
your golden skin
reflects the night

a night of love/a night of passion
you have had so many
       that you do not know what they mean

and when nothing does not mean anything
the lies are spoken in truth
the rhythm sounds
and you know the answer
       that there is no answer at all

as she grabbed me in passion
the passion became only a game
in a game
like in all games
someone wins/someone loses
and someone gets up and walks away

       what a life…
       my life

thirty-eight

I could not say that passion swept her eyes
for it was much too dark to see what they had to say
but into the darkness she melted softly

      dark-to-dark
          into the night

and by her touch
I could not say
if she truly loved me
it came on like a gentle wave
that held me tight in its embrace
as it slowly pulled me out to sea

      the sea
      where a drop of water merges
          into the infinite
          becoming one
          a part of the whole
          never to be singular again
          never to be known again

          like her
          never to be seen again

thirty-nine

as I wait…
the moments tick by
staring at the pale green walls

    these moments are gone

waiting
for a desire
a desire of desirelessness
a dream
that has not yet been lived
I wait
staring at a pale green wall
and a T.V.

    a moment…

forty

I am ready to fall asleep
fall asleep
in blitzed out
   bangkok drunken stupor

a night of dance
a night of song
my head spins

forty-one

yes, I danced with them
danced them into the ground
as good as they were
they could not hold up/hold a candle
to the American dance of freedom
passee'
now-a-days
punk rock style

yes, I danced with you tonight
bangkok woman
who had a tail in her hair

      let me explain for those of you
      of a different space/a different time
      a tail: a long thin strand of hair
      hanging from the back of the head
      worn in the west in the late 70s
      and early 80s
      attributed to the punk rock era
      once upon a time, I wore one too…

yes, I danced with you
but I returned to my room tonight
      returned to it alone

      alone from friends
      alone from love
      alone from sex
      as my head spins
          spins
          spins
          spins

now, I could have loved you
a woman who steps out of sync

      steps out of sync
      in bangkok time

but my head
it spins too hard
so I danced with you
and then just said goodnight

      a night
            another gone by
      in bangkok
      and *my nights of drunken stupor*

      another night
      where the fool I am
      drank them under the table
      danced them into the floor
      and walked out of the room
      in all my style

      alone

forty-two

my head spins
my ears ring
and I want to throw-up

I danced
danced and drank
        the night away
and what could it prove

        another lie
        in a life
        of time/of space/of reality

I turn my attentions
        to tomorrow night
when the spin will have slowed
and new dreams
well, they are always present

forty-three

I doze off as I stare
I stare at the emptiness
that is inside of me

       of the love of life
       that I do not hold

at a life that is almost complete
yet so incomplete

stare in the right direction
       it is impossible not to see

       this is it
       thailand

I have looked so far
I have been here so many times
crept deeply into this pagan dream
ran quickly from this pagan lie
for where does the reality exist
in this battle to keep hold of it

I have battled so long
battled since I was thirteen years, maybe fourteen
now here I sit, thailand
I am twenty-seven
older than many/younger than some
living truth/living lies
it is all thailand
you hold me here

I spin
I fall asleep

54

as I sit here on the floor
leaning against my bed
you come to my dreams again
thai goddess in human skin
untouched flower
in a virgin garden
the dream brings tears to my eyes

I cry in the night
I cry as I sleep
for you I have longed for such a time
Asian dream
of my Asian days
golden goddess when will I be allowed
to touch your feet

I wake to the sun
crawl from the floor into my bed
let my head that hurts
        fade to the distant daydreams
of what is to come
of the dreams that will be lived
when I finally find you
walking down a distant street
        in a distant dream
        of unlived fantasies
        in which we may embrace

until I find you
I will chase your vision

forty-four

it is a funny dream
it is a funny fantasy
waiting until the alcohol runs out
waiting until the alcohol wears off

as my mind clears
      my eyes clear
and I see myself
in the vision of a woman
another woman
I do not know her name
I see my reflection in her eyes

      a reflection of a fool
      seen in a fool's vision

forty-five

casual rejection
it is hard to take
when there is only
one person in the place worth dancing with
and she is with another man

forty-six

there was this dude
      he was dressed like a chick
      acted like a chick
      looked like a chick
      yeah, I almost dicked him

      lost time of lost life
      lost time of lost mind
      where my vision is so clouded
      my wisdom so unclear

but me, I grew up in Hollywood
L.A. born and raised
and thank god
for the knowledge of the streets
the knowledge of the unseen
the eyes to see the illusion
to know that what is there
      is not really there
what is seen
      is not always what is felt

through double-vision sight
I detected a fault
in the perfection of a willing face
in the night
and I am glad that I chose
another dancing partner
for had my desire not been so strong
or had my sight not been so clear
I would have gotten to my room
discovered the illusion
and I would have had to kick
that fucking drag queens ass

58

forty-seven

do you think about me tonight
thailand lady

      I think not

do you remember me

      maybe, but I doubt it

but that is sad
for so few think
and so few have a meaning

but behind it all
is this mystic's illusion

why don't you step into it
you know that you have nothing left to lose

forty-eight

I look through physical eyes
I see physical things
I desire physical pleasures
am I so different than anyone else ?

> will you meet me tomorrow night
> > I think so
> will you demonstrate your knowledge
> > no doubt

> but all I have to offer in return is my truth
> > which is fully ridden with lies

> payment and return
> for I have nothing to get up for
> no real reason to be

> businessmen/familymen
> now they have a reason
> > a reason to believe

but I looked at all their ways
seen it from the outside in
touched the desire
felt the lack of desire
it is all the same
simply falsehood
that the self feeds to itself
so me, I am a drifter
moving around the world
and I love bangkok
bangkok, I see that you need yourself
I wonder if you need me

forty-nine

I guess today is the 26th
but I have always wondered just what that meant

today I saw the monks walking
      once I lived among them
      I listened to those
      who thought that they knew
            but what
                  in fact
                  do they really know ?

    each line
    in its place
          placed in its proper place

    all things expected/all things organized

    maybe a reality/maybe a condition

but me, I prefer this
      to the lines
      that never lose their place

and you know
I have heard so many words spoken
lies spoken as truths

      spoken as the way
          the only way

by those who have laid claim to know

but me, I am out here on the outskirts
alone and drunk in thailand

now I could have chosen
the other path
      the road of being holy

     so pure/so true

the way all the religious men
throughout eternity
have preached their way
as the only way

but a dance is just a dance
and we all are just the same

for those who claim to know
      never really know
          and the only truth is silence

      it is now 3:14 A.M.
      but I have often wondered
      just what that meant

as the space
turns into space
it blends into something more
and where there is everything
there is always nothing
it is lurking
around the next turn

fifty

so few ever know the reality
of getting totally fucked up
in a foreign land

   pure mysticism

where there is no-where to go
and you don't know your way home
and you are stuck there
with only yourself

nirvana comes is strange forms

fifty-one

wake up and lick my wounds
      from living
           the night before

     head spins
     stomach turns
     neck is sore
     legs are sore
     I have been down this read
     one too many times

so the daylight it has come
it dances its way in
      a day that should be spent
          asleep
          licking my wounds
          but I awake
          and desire-full

fifty-two

getting onto the airplane
bound for a northern thai town
     she,
     a beautiful,
     oh so beautiful
     thai girl
     looks at me
     her newlywed arab husband
     his eyes
     they burn with jealousy

     both have found a new passion
     his, his jealousy
     hers, her realization
     that perhaps her decision
     was not the right one

yes, had you been free
yes, had you been alone
and yes, had you looked at me
with those eyes of lustful love
     I would have held you long
          I would have held you tight
Instead, you carried
     two thai boarding passes
     for two thai seats
          one next to the other
               two just the same

you were not alone
but in your mind/I could see it in your eyes
you questioned whether or not
you had made the right decision
whether life had given you the right choice

there I was
tall, long blond locks
of California skin
California ocean blood

a man with no reason
but full of illusion
and a game filled dream to live

a choice was made
but where do our choices come from
they come from availability

a meeting/a moment
a woman/a man
a moment of the right movement
in a hot thai night

what is never known
is what new choices may come
what may present itself
farther down the line

I know in that moment
you questioned
I know, for I have questioned many times myself
that is what keeps me up
keeps me dancing

with every dance
there is another chance

for any choice that is made
where there is a question
is only the choice of a fool

and so we both looked at each other
and realized
had it been a different time/in a different moment
in a seemingly different world
we would have touched

but now
it is only cast to a memory
cast to a dreamer's written lines
cast to the shadows
of the thailand clouds
shadows of the thailand sky

fifty-three

thai woman
some I see
others I touch
a few I choose to love

but like everywhere
few ever gain the vision
to step into
a dream-filled
mystic's illusion

ah, what a dance…

fifty-four

when you look in the clouds
have you forgotten to see what is there
    what shapes move
    what shapes become
    what shapes dance
        in a child-like mind

have the clouds
simply become the clouds
    nothing more
    nothing to become

do you have to force yourself
to see the shapes/see the dreams
    make something
    knowing that you must…
        or can you just feel
        feel the dream

lay back
remember
remember the dream

fifty-five

old monk
obviously one since youth
he walked into a famous temple
temple of a famous shrine
I took his picture
I bowed to him
he smiled
came over
and shook my hand

fifty-six

you move to me
ask me into your car
nighttime eyes
shut down
oh, you're good
oh, you're fine
if you weren't a whore
I would probably marry you

       but in the space
       and in the distance
       the space between the lines
       there exists a void
       of such persistence
       never will it let you go

       in the hills
       in the streets
       the smell it drives you mad
       from the pace
       of the distant persistence
       your nighttime eyes
       they could shut me down

but me
I bang my head
I smash it against the wall
all the lines/all the lies
they have all gone too far

       I have heard them all before

you hold my hand
so close/so long

you are an expert
at your craft

but my distant eyes of loneliness
they see the same in yours

I listen to you as you speak
your promises that will never be
but you keep your pace
      a whore
           who keeps her distance
           in here persistence
           a lie to live
           and a love to feel

you come to me
ask me in
your nighttime eyes are so fine
you hold me close
you hold me long
I would probably marry you
but you are just a whore

fifty-seven

I feel so far away
      it feels so far away

I have taken so many long steps
I have come here
directed by the signs
yet, I remain lost in the distance

      the distance
      to have taken so many steps
      to find it
      and the only understanding is that
      there are too many steps
      to ever return home

fifty-eight

today she held me close
I could have taken her
I wanted to take her
      to touch
      to be touched by her
      thailand beauty
      yet in my own desire(s)
      I froze

today I could have left
for a new land
      another distant face
      in another distant place
bound for it
all alone
yet, I did not
I chose to remain

      incoming and outgoing
      it is simply a point of view
      in one moment
      I have learned to take new steps
      in the next
      I am afraid to move

it doesn't really matter
I know what I have done
it is all just lived
for so short a time
and then it is gone

      lost, so lost
      in desire

lost, so lost
in living the dream

the hole that is created
leaves the emptiness that remains

many have spoken the same words
many have written the same lines
some pretend to know it
some pretend that it does not exist
but it does

so a kiss hello
       leads to the kiss goodbye

and when there is no movement
       nothing is lost
       and nothing is gained
       but in the heart of emptiness
       the truth unfolds

fifty-nine

now
I become the warrior
as I dance
into the arena of lies

now
I prepare for battle
in the dance
I know very well

>   my eyes are keen
>   my ears listen to the sound
>   there is a fluctuation in the tone
>   I believe my senses
>   but who will emerge the victor
>   in a battle
>   that I did not choose

I dress myself for combat
the warrior in me shines
my mind clear
my spirit strong
I am ready
I have become the warrior

the battle is prepared for
with the dance
moves the new chance
and in the moment of confrontation
I will go for the throat

sixty

two nights in bangkok
the two nights that I knew you for
        holding you
        sleeping with you
        making love with you

        known for only a moment
        but how I miss your golden skin
        your almost Asian eyes

how I long to hold you tonight
as we both softly cry

        yes, I love you
        there is no doubt

        but then love
        it never seems to last
        not, very long
        not, anyway…

sixty-one

     touched
     felt

I dragged you from vague illusion
into passionate romance
a love that gave you a reason
to throw everything else away

     I touched you
     I left

     you know the words
     you have spoken
         the lies
             can't you see
             that they are all so cheap

     cheap as tears
     in the crushing force
     of *too long in thailand*
     the punch of the bangkok night
     in which we met

if you spoke better english
or if I spoke better thai
then you may have fallen into
my mystic daydream

but as few words were spoken
few words remain unsaid
you simply fell in love with me
love as it was/love as it is
only for a moment

and if I had a promise to keep
I would definitely make it to you
and if there were any reason
to continue this lie
I would be sure that you knew it too

I do not know the pretense
I guess I don't even care
all I know
is the flow of the dance
the dance that brought you next to me

what can I do but live it

sixty-two

you know you stepped over the line for me
something I will never forget
you came back
you knocked on my door
and you asked me
if the sign was true
Do Not Disturb

no, I said
come in

sixty-three

slowly I die in this place
each day
        a step closer

the moments
they become short
and I do not know what to do

I could leave,
        you know
I have a ticket

but instead I stay
        each day
        facing the inevitable
        a moment shorter
        a step closer

I stay for this love
        a dream…

is it a given gift of the goddess

I could go/I should go
but I stay
stay for this woman
this gift/this lie of love

        each moment
        I step
        a step closer
        as I slowly, ever so slowly
        begin to die

sixty-four

I look at her
I fall in love
> I touch her
> and my love grows

> in love
> yes we are

> this love
> a total sacrifice
> for her/for me

I look at my life
what I have in L.A.
I look at what I am living
here in thailand
and I know
that there is no better place
for me to be

> bangkok
> > *to be dying slowly...*

sixty-five

Mick sits in a hundred dollar hotel room
mine is two hundred bills, U.S.
poor Mick

romance sitting over the Chao Praya
       no turning back
       it plays loudly in my ears

love sits down
reading a letter
that I wrote to her
a few days before
from Taipei
       it just arrived

romance, it isn't too bad

she tells me
if I had not returned
the letter would have no meaning
well, I did come back
Southeast Asia and the dream

romance, it isn't too bad
but it is a fool's game

sixty-six

love – lost again
lost within its bounds
lust – tasted again
neither ever seem to last

but I have driven so deeply into both
        lived so long
        lasted so short a time

yet, I always am the fool
who keeps coming back for more
yes, I am the fool
        who lets love momentarily steal my space
        steal my time
        even steal my money
but love, when it is love
oh, it feels so good
and lust, when it is really lust
nothing can touch the sensation

        love and lust
        do they ever meet
        only for a moment or two
                the love of lust
                or the lust of love
                two roads that take you
                to the same place
yes, I have fallen in
fallen in again
but it feels so good
yes, I am a fool
isn't it amazing
how drunken passion
turn into intoxicated love

sixty-seven

me
well, I have danced into this destiny
        into some sort of truth
        but a truth
        that has stabbed me in the heart

                the ultimate truth
                        where no answers lie

        and me, I am tired
        so tired of this truth

        I look over the thai mountains
        they speak a different tongue
        could I live here forever

        forever
        such a short time…

sixty-eight

the space
the space that calls
the space between the lines
the space where two worlds collide
soul-to-soul
and a heart touches a heart
a moment into totality
a moment of love
a feeling
that can only be held back
by the loss of the moment
a dance
a dance into separation
a dance into suchness
where no one knows
if the end justifies the means
only a chance can be taken

      yes, I love you
      no reason
      simply that I do

passed onto the intro-flections
passed to the demons
      of culture and time

a step to the left/a step to the right
      both leading to nowhere
      nowhere
      being the only place to remain

I have danced in your love
I have held you so tight

waiting only for the new morning
when I can again wake
and see your closed eyes

into the world
of the unforgiven
lost to moment in the past

      cast to demon cells
          of lost demon hells
          into the world of true romance

sixty-nine

if it were any other city
      any city
      one step closer in time

      tokyo
      taipei
      singapore
      even hong kong

I would stay with you forever
but bangkok
      what a mess
I have been here too long
it weights heavy on my mind
I must leave

seventy

bangkok
I have returned
it is almost hard to believe
but I believe in the space
I believe in the dream
I believe in your lies
a kiss awaits me
a kiss tonight
> she had to go to her car
> she had forgotten something
> and I…
> I sit here alone
> I am present
> in all my traveler-ness
> surrounded by tourists
> *there is a difference, you know*
> I hope
> I will not be confused with them
> but a kiss brought me back
> a lived total illusion
> in a lived total night
why do I return ?
because there is no way out
no in between
only total essence
that can be lived
here in bangkok
> a step onto the edge
> the step that keeps me coming back for more
> I have returned so many times
> a step
> this time
> that may well throw me over the edge

seventy-one

we sit here
staring into each others eyes
a reason to dream/a reason to be confused
all the reason to live

but a kiss
it is all too short
and age comes upon us all
and so I live while I can

> *passive pagan illusion*
> *in a passionate bangkok night*

> all the reasons to love
>   and all the reasons to die

seventy-two

a road to paradise
a road into the abyss
a road of promised passion
and forgotten love
a road that lies
too far ahead
and is far too dark

seventy-three

coffee, wine, and women
kisses in a Siam dream
      passion burns
      like a passion flower
a flower blooming
in a silent and secret
bangkok night

and you know it was so easy
but it hasn't always been that way
      high heels
        and fashion passion
they stagger in the back of my mind

coffee, wine, and women
cheap roses in Siam's spinning night

bangkok kisses me
with my thai destiny

      it is all a big kiss
      a passionate kiss
      goodnight

seventy-four

british music videos on a T.V.
a bangkok street scene
out the window
to my side
my thai love
sitting next to me
another java, if you please…

I sit here watching life
        as it goes by

how many times I have realized
that this could be heaven
that this could be anywhere
anywhere in the world
but it is gladly only thailand
where any dream will do

seventy-five

high heels
        and tight blue jean pants
I have to tell
        you look like a cheap whore

I mean where is the fashion
        the long skirts
        the classic look
        that I love so much

but no
you prefer
to dress like you think
Americans dress

but I have to tell you
the American ladies don't dress that way

        casual compassion
                and fatal fashion

I have to bite my pride
to be seen with you

seventy-six

love, lust, and possibilities
as I have never realized before

where were my eyes/where was my mind

all those other times in thailand

but my eyes
they have opened
and my desire
it has peaked
and I realize the beauty
        of the golden goddess
the beauty
        that has always been with me

and that I never before noticed before...

seventy-seven

a beautiful thai whore
asked me to dance tonight
as I sat all alone
drinking a *Perrier*

I turned her down
and it doing so
somehow a million years
of good karma
was built up
and a million years
of bad karma
was washed away

seventy-eight

out here on the extremities
        passion, it is not cheap
out here on the far side
        nothing comes for free

for every price paid
        something is somehow returned
and for all the greed shown
        something is also lost

bangkok, you have the kiss
        that can only be known by so few
bangkok, the price for your knowledge
        it is so high

                I have paid
                        and I have played
all the time
I have known you inside and out

I love you
        like so few have loved you
        and you have stabbed me in the heart

but from all that is lost
        something is also gained
and so for all I have given you
        you have returned
                me living your dream

I always come back to you
it seems I can never stay away
I have watched you change
as times have changed

the change has not always been good to you
but, nothing can ever stay the same
      certainly not you or I

thailand
to me you have given me the goddess
      a green goddess of certainly
      a golden goddess of love

so tonight, is a last night
but it will give birth to the new
      a kiss of passion
      a kiss of love
      I will count the moment
      until my return

out here on the extremities
passion it does not come cheap
but when the only passion
is the loved passion
a kiss is always returned

seventy-nine

the night air is warm
in the radio station
and we are left alone
the music
we place it on tape
to be played tomorrow

      tomorrow is always another day

we sit
her and I
and we dog down

china white
but this is thailand
where illusion reigns supreme

peachy is her name
the princess of bangkok radio
pichitra, on her U.S. passport
a name given her by the queen

      the queen of thailand
      no lie

but now she has developed a passion
      it is an unbreakable spell
      it leads here from one day to the next

      pong kow
      it is called
      or simply, *powder white*

one minute spreads to the next
        for soon she must be home
children to take care of
a thai husband to love
but for now it is simply the moment
        a moment
        in which I watch her eyes spin

        her eyes spin
        my eyes spin
        an embrace of illusion
        an embrace of the best kind
        as she reveals to me
        all of her secrets
        all of her truths

here-and-now
it is all that matters
bangkok radio simply pays the bills

the bills for a white princess
in a golden land
who's desire of illusion
sends her into the best
of what bangkok has to offer
white powder ma

hello bangkok
this is rock'n hollywood scott
and my good friend peachy tells me
that we are going to pick up the pace here a little bit
with a band from my home-town of L.A.
but remember bangkok
when you wanta play
you gotta pay

eighty

it was a kiss that held me long
it was a kiss that held me hard
it made me come back for more

      more of what
          was the only question

a fool diving into
     his paradise

      the afternoon was beautiful
      the clouds formed images in the sky
      the Chao Praya River flowed
      down below us
      as we made love
          hotel passion

a fool diving into
his paradise

      she told me
      how much she loved me
      I told here
      how much I didn't care
      she told me
      how there had never been
      anyone like me before
      no doubt, was my answer

lost in momentary lust
a fool diving into his paradise

but somehow the truth
fights to come out

it always has on me
her lies of love
and her dreams awaiting
through they sucked me in
the wave sucked out on her

for in a moment of silence
the truths to me were told
and all I could do
was to laugh to myself
            at the money spent
            the moments stolen
            and the lies
            that I longer to believe

        a free whore
                is never cheap

a fool who dove
into his fool's paradise

eighty-one

in our moments
oh yes, we did love
but love never seems to last

in the dance
      the dance of time
      everything always changes

      I searched all of the bangkok booksellers
      to find this special text
      the tao te ching
            when I found it
            I wrote in it, I love you
            I gave it to her
            in the bangkok evening air

but as things change
sometimes they slap you in the face
and when the lies come in
sometimes it is true that the pursuit of nothingness
means more than having everything

      to the man of the world
      everyday something is gained
      to the man of Tao
      everyday something is lost

her chain of lies
became broken
who and what she really was…
one night, it was told to me

so, in the book,
I simply crossed out the words
    I love you
I left the book with her
     in her car

    a reminder of the time
    a reminder of the lies
    a laughing note to myself
    in a life so well orchestrated

hey, no big thing, you know…
I have told a momentary lover
       a lie or thirty myself

eighty-two

it is a funny way in
        to find a way out
when you become trapped
under the weight of love

no way in/no way out
only the knowledge
that it cannot last too long

so when any reason
        is reason enough
and lies they come to light
I thank the reason
for the living treason
I thank them for a way out

eighty-three

a glass of champagne
        the most expensive on the menu
I watch
        while she tilted it to her lips
could she taste the difference
        I don't think so, no
but the taste it left with her
        how could she ever forget

I undress her
        I lay her down
in an elegant hotel suite
        I make love to her
slowly, passionately
        can she feel the difference
no doubt that she can

but when all the lessons are taught
and all the money is spent
when the sex becomes old and expected
as with anyone/everyone
can there be anything left ?

like a chunk of clay/like a white canvas
once something is created
it belongs only to the artist
a possession by any other name

eighty-four

if there were trees to climb
certainly, I would climb them
if there were mountains to walk
I would go to the top of them
but this is the city
dirty/overcrowded
filled with minds that dream
of other places
          dream of other ways

so all that is left
is swamp fields to look at
but never run through
boats to ride on the rivers
but never swim in
and expensive hotel rooms to rent
and fill with as much
golden skinned passion
as possible

though I love it
I hate it too
my mind goes on
          to other places
other realms
far less fatal
than bangkok

eighty-five

deal me in
I play any game
      win or lose
      who cares
it won't be me
who will cry any tears

meet me tonight
      kiss me
      oh yes, kiss me
      nothing else really matters

          just tonight

yes, it is me
I will tilt a glass or two

yes, it is me
I will love you
oh yes, I will love you

and when it is all gone
I'll be gone

and any game you play/any card you deal
      I won't cry any tears

      tears are much too meaningless

eighty-six

sound and night
moved into the lights
silence, I need silence

there isn't any fear
      none to believe in
strength is all
      all that is given me

      as I walk back
      back, into the bangkok night

eighty-seven

your golden ways did not bind me
        they gave me passage
        back to the night

your kisses did not hypnotize me
        just a lie to a lie

any loss
        is any gain
so you go back to drinking your cheap whiskey
I'll go back to my champagne

my heart is filled with our promises
        promises for another lady
        in another night
        another golden body
        pressed tightly
        against mine

eighty-eight

passion stalks
until the love is trapped
unleashed your fierce fury upon me
I see you/I have you
        you are mine

passion in its cage

eighty-nine

of all the time here
of all the feelings known
of all the loves lost
of all the loves gained

        lust
        love
        loss
        gain
        intoxication
        distance

        the nothing that equals nothing

        the pleasure/the pain

I leave
and I an left, continually
        with a reason to return

I can never get away from you bangkok
I am never too far from your grasp

ninety

bangkok
this strangely
creative
poetic
space

s.
1984 – 1986
bangkok, thailand

.

Scott Shaw's *Books-In-Print* include:

The Little Book of Yoga Breathing,
Nirvana in a Nutshell,
About Peace: 108 Ways to Be At Peace
      When Things Are Out of Control,
Zen O'clock: Time To Be,
The Tao of Self Defense,
Samurai Zen,
The Ki Process: Korean Secrets
      for Cultivating Dynamic Energy,
The Warrior is Silent:
      Martial Arts and the Spiritual Path,
Hapkido: The Korean Art of Self Defense,
Taekwondo Basics,
Advanced Taekwondo,
Chi Kung For Beginners,
Mastering Health: The A to Z of Chi Kung,
Cambodia Refugees in Long Beach, California,
China Deep,
Essence: The Zen of Everything,
Hapkido: Essays on Self-Defense,
Shanghai Whispers Shanghai Screams,
Shattered Thoughts,
Junk: The Back Streets of Bangkok,
The Passionate Kiss of Illusion,
TKO: Lost Nights in Tokyo,
Zen Buddhism: The Pathway to Nirvana,
Zen: Tales from the Journey,
Zen in the Blink of an Eye,
Yoga: A Spiritual Guidebook,
Marguerite Duras and Charles Bukowski: The Yin
      and Yang of Modern Erotic Literature.

www.ingramcontent.com/pod-product-compliance
Lightning Source LLC
Chambersburg PA
CBHW060413090426
42734CB00011B/2305